OUTLINE OF THE VEDANTA SYSTEM OF PHILOSOPHY

ACCORDING TO SHANKARA

OUTLINE OF THE VEDANTA SYSTEM OF PHILOSOPHY

ACCORDING TO SHANKARA

BY PAUL DEUSSEN

TRANSLATED BY J. H. WOODS

AND C. B. RUNKLE

GYAN

Published by

GYAN

Gyan Publishing House
5, Ansari Road
Daryaganj, New Delhi-110002
Phone: 011-47034999, 9811692060
E-mail: books@gyanbooks.com

Distribution Network
gyanbooks.com
India, USA, Canada, UK, Australia

ISBN: 978-93-6208-142-1 (HB)
First Published, 1906

2nd Impression 2024

Printed at: Gyan Press, Delhi.

OUTLINE OF THE VEDANTA SYSTEM OF PHILOSOPHY ACCORDING TO SHANKARA

Author: PAUL DEUSSEN, TRANSLATOR: J. H. WOODS AND C. B. RUNKLE

OUTLINE OF THE VEDANTA

OUTLINE OF THE VEDANTA SYSTEM OF PHILOSOPHY

ACCORDING TO SHANKARA

By PAUL DEUSSEN

PROFESSOR OF PHILOSOPHY AT THE UNIVERSITY OF KIEL

Translated by J. H. WOODS

INSTRUCTOR IN PHILOSOPHY AT HARVARD UNIVERSITY

and C. B. RUNKLE

OF CAMBRIDGE, MASSACHUSETTS

NEW YORK

THE GRAFTON PRESS

70 FIFTH AVENUE

CONTENTS

PREFATORY NOTE

BY THE AUTHOR

ON *the tree of Indian wisdom there is no fairer flower than the Upanishads, and no finer fruit than the Vedānta philosophy. This system grew out of the teachings of the Upanishads, and was brought to its consummate form by the great Shankara (born 788* A.D.*, exactly one thousand years before his spiritual kinsman Schopenhauer). Even to this day, Shankara's system represents the common belief of nearly all thoughtful Hindus, and deserves to be widely studied in the Occident. To the end that it might be so studied, I published more than twenty years ago a compendium of the system, under the title* "Das System des Vedānta" *(Leipzig: F. A Brockhaus, 1883), and at the close of the work, I added a brief outline of Shankara's doctrine.*

The translation of that outline was submitted to me by my friend and for some time disciple in Germany, Dr. James H. Woods, after his return from Benares. I have read and revised it with care, and suggested some changes and additions; and I trust that it may prove to be of service in acquainting American students with Shankara.

PAUL DEUSSEN

Kiel, November 18, 1905

Abbreviations

BAU. = Bṛhad Āraṇyaka Upanishad
ChU. = Chāndogya Upanishad
ÇvetU. = Çvetaçvatara Upanishad
Içā. = Īçā Upanishad
KU. = Kena Upanishad
KshU. = Kaushītaki Upanishad
KthU. = Kāṭhaka Upanishad
MuU. = Muṇḍaka Upanishad
PU. = Praçna Upanishad
Ts. = Taittirīya-samhitā

OUTLINE OF THE VEDANTA SYSTEM OF PHILOSOPHY

CHAPTER I

INTRODUCTION

THE fundamental idea of the Vedānta system, as most tersely expressed in the words of the Veda, "That art thou" (*tat tvam asi*[1]), and "I am Brahman" (*aham brahma asmi*[2]), is the identity of Brahman and the soul. This means that Brahman, that is, the eternal principle of all being, the power which creates all worlds, sustains them and again absorbs them, is identical with the Ātman, the self, or the soul; namely, with that in us which, when we judge rightly, we acknowledge as our own self, as our inner and true essence. This soul in each one of us is not a part of Brahman nor an emanation from him, but it is, fully and entirely, the eternal indivisible Brahman itself.

Fundamental idea of the system

2. This assertion contradicts experience,[3] which presents not any such unity, but rather a multiplicity,[4] a complex[5] of names and forms,[6] and as a part of these, our Self, incorporated in our body which has come into being and must in time be disintegrated.

Contradicted by experience

[1] *ChU. vi.* 8.7. [2] *BAU. i.* 4.10. [3] Vyavahāra.
[4] Nānātva. [5] Prapañca. [6] Nāmarūpe, *that is, impressions of the ear and of the eye, sense-perceptions.*

3. No less the fundamental assumption of the Vedānta system contradicts the canon of the Vedic ritual: this indeed assumes a survival[7] of the self beyond the body; but it also presupposes a multiplicity of individual souls discrete from Brahman. These souls, engaged in an endless round-of-rebirth,[8] enter one body after another, the deeds[9] done in each life necessarily determining the succeeding life and its quality.

Contradiction of the Vedic ritual

4. Experience, as it is the result of our perceptive and cognitive faculties,[10] and the Vedic ritual as well, with its commands and prohibitions, its promises and threats, both rest on a false cognition,[11] an innate illusion,[12] called *avidyā* or ignorance, the assertions of which, like apparitions in a dream, are true only till one awakes. On closer inquiry this innate *avidyā* is found to consist in the fact that the *ātman*, that is, the soul, the self, is not able to distinguish itself from the *upādhis* or limiting conditions with which it is invested. These limiting conditions include the body, the physical organs, and the deeds; and only a part of them, namely, the body, is destroyed at death, the rest accompanying the soul in its transmigrations. The converse of this *avidyā* is knowledge (*vidyā*), also called right cognition or universal

Ignorance and knowledge

[7] Vyatireka. [8] Saṁsāra. [9] Karman.
[10] Pramāṇa, *including immediate apprehension* (pratyaṣka), *inference* (anumāna), *and so forth.* [11] Mithyā-jñāna. [12] Bhrānti.

cognition,[13] by virtue of which the *ātman* distinguishes himself from the *upādhis*, and recognizes that the latter, resting on *avidyā*, are mere illusion[14] or erroneous assumption,[15] whereas he himself is identical with the one and only one, the all-embracing Brahman.

5 Universal cognition[16] cannot be attained by means of worldly perceptive and cognitive faculties,[17] nor can it be enjoined as a duty by the canonical ordinances of the Veda, because both of these have their origin in *avidyā* and cannot lead beyond it. The source of knowledge

The sole source of *vidyā* is rather revelation, (*çruti* (or Scripture, as we not very appropriately translate it). By *çruti* is meant the Veda, both its "Work-section and Knowledge-section,"[18] the latter including several chapters scattered through the Mantras and Brāhmaṇas, and especially the concluding chapters of the Brāhmaṇas called the Veda-end (*Veda-anta*, that is, *Vedānta*) or Upanishads. The entire Veda, including both Work-section and Knowledge-section, the whole body of the Mantras (hymns and sacrificial formulas), the Brāhmaṇas (theological expositions), and the Upanishads, is of divine origin. It was "breathed forth" by Brahman, and only "seen" by the human authors, the inspired sages or Rishis. The world, including the gods, passes away, but

[13] Saṁyag-darçana. [14] Māyā. [15] Abhimāna.
[16] Saṁyag-darçana, *literally, cognition which converges from all sides to one point.* [17] *See paragraph* 4. [18] Karma-kāṇḍa *and* jñāna-kāṇḍa.

the Veda is eternal; it survives the destruction of the universe and continues to exist in the soul of Brahman. In accordance with the word of the Veda which contains the eternal archetypes of all things, gods, men, animals, and so forth, are created anew by Brahman at the beginning of each world-cycle. The Veda is then revealed to them by the breath of Brahman. The Work-section is revealed as a code of conduct having happiness[19] as its object; the Knowledge-section, as the source of right cognition,[20] the one and only fruit of which is blessedness,[21] that is, emancipation. Not by reflection[22] is right cognition to be attained, nor yet through tradition or *smṛti.*[23] Both reflection and tradition can only in a secondary sense be considered the source of truth, namely, in so far as, being based on the Veda, they attempt to interpret and supplement its revelation.

19 Abhyudaya.

20 Saṁyag-darçana.

21 Niḥçreyasa, *the summum bonum.*

22 Tarka.

23 Smṛti *includes the Vedic Sūtras, the Sāṁkhya and Yoga systems, the Law-book of Manu, the Mahābhārata, and so forth.*

CHAPTER II

THEOLOGY

6. THE supreme aim of human beings[1] is emancipation,[2] that is, the cessation of the soul's transmigrations;[3] but this emancipation of the soul from its transmigrations is brought about by the recognition of the individual self,[4] as identical with the highest Self,[5] namely, Brahman. The entire content of *vidyā* is, consequently, knowledge of the *Ātman* or *Brahman*, for the two concepts are interchangeable.

Esoteric and exoteric science

There are, however, two kinds of knowledge in reference to Brahman, the higher[6] and the lower[7] knowledge. The higher knowledge has for its object right cognition,[8] and its one and only fruit is emancipation; the lower knowledge does not aim at knowledge of Brahman, but at his worship,[9] and has as its fruit, according to the grade of worship, success in undertakings,[10] happiness,[11] and finally progressive emancipation.[12] The object of the higher knowledge is the higher Brahman;[13] of the lower knowledge, the lower Brahman.[14]

7. The Veda, then, distinguishes two forms[15] of Brah-

[1] Puruṣa-artha. [2] Mokṣa. [3] Saṁsāra.
[4] Ātman. [5] Parama-ātman. [6] Parā vidyā.
[7] Aparā vidyā. [8] Saṁyag-darçana. [9] Upāsanā.
[10] Karma-samṛddhi.
[11] Abhyudaya, *in heaven, or perhaps in the succeeding birth.*
[12] Kramamukti. [13] Param brahma. [14] Aparam brahma.
[15] Rūpe.

man: the higher, attributeless[16] Brahman; and the lower Brahman, possessing attributes.[17] As to the former, the Veda teaches that Brahman is devoid of all attributes,[18] distinctions,[19] forms,[20] and limiting conditions.[21] To the latter, for purposes of worship, it ascribes various attributes, distinctions, forms, and conditions.

Esoteric and exoteric Brahman

8. One and the same object cannot be with and without attributes, with and without form in itself.[22] Brahman is without attributes, form, difference, and limitation, but becomes the lower Brahman when ignorance[23] imposes on it, for the purpose of worship, the limiting conditions or *upadhis*. The imposition on Brahman of *upādhis* is only an illusion, just as it is an illusion to look upon a crystal as red when it reflects a red colour. As the transparency of the crystal is not affected by the red colour, so the essence of Brahman is not changed by the limiting conditions imposed upon it by *avidyā*.

Difference between esoteric and exoteric

9. The higher Brahman is, in essence, without attributes,[24] formless,[25] devoid of distinctions,[26] and unconditioned.[27] It is "not gross and not subtile, not short and not long,"[28] and so forth; "not to be heard, not to be touched, formless,

The esoteric Brahman is unknowable

[16] Para, nirguṇa. [17] Apara, saguṇa. [18] Guṇa.
[19] Viçeṣa. [20] Akāra. [21] Upādhī. [22] Svatas.
[23] Avidyā. [24] Nirguṇa. [25] Nirākāra.
[26] Nirviçeṣa. [27] Nirupādhika. [28] *BAU. iii.* 8.8.

imperishable;"[29] it is "not so and not so,"[30] that is, no form and no representation can express its essence. It is therefore "different from that which we know and from that which we do not know;"[31] words and thoughts turn back from it without finding it;[32] and Bāhva, the sage, answered the question regarding its essence by silence.[33]

Nature of esoteric Brahman

10. The only thing that can be predicated of the attributeless Brahman is that it is not non-existent. It is therefore The Existent (*Sat*); but from the empirical point of view Brahman is rather the Non-Existent. The Scriptures still further define the essence of Brahman by declaring that, as a lump of salt has the taste of salt throughout, so Brahman is throughout pure intelligence.[34] In these assertions, two attributes are not ascribed to Brahman, since both are identical; for the essence of being consists in intelligence; that of intelligence, in being. Bliss (*ānanda*)[35] is occasionally acknowledged as a predicate of the attributeless Brahman, but it is not mentioned in the discussion of its essence, perhaps because it is considered a

29 *KthU. i.* 3.15. 30 Neti, neti, *BAU. ii.* 3.6. 31 *KU. i.* 3.

32 *TS. ii.* 4.

33 *When Vāshkali bade Bāhva teach him Brahman, the sage explained it to him by silence. He said to him, "Learn Brahman, O friend," and became silent. When questioned the second and the third time, he replied, "I am teaching you indeed, but you do not understand. Silent is that Self." See Shankara on Vedānta Sūtra, iii.* 2.17.

34 Cāitanya.

35 *The later Vedānta attributes* ānanda *to Brahman as a third predicate under the name* Sac-cid-ānanda.

merely negative quality, that is, as freedom from pain. Of Brahman alone can freedom from pain be predicated; for the Scripture saith, "All that is different from Brahman,—*that* is subject to pain."[36]

Intuitive cognition of esoteric Brahman as Soul

11. The impossibility of cognizing the attributeless Brahman rests on the fact that Brahman is the inner Self[37] in everything that exists. As such it is more certain than anything else and cannot be denied by any one; but, on the other hand, it is impossible to cognize it, because in every act of cognition it is the knowing subject and therefore never an object. Brahman is, however, perceived by the sage in the state of *saṁrādhana*, complete satisfaction, which consists in the withdrawing the organs of sense from everything external, and in concentrating them upon one's own inner nature. In the consciousness that our inner Self is the attributeless Brahman, and in the accompanying conviction of the non-reality of the whole complex of names and forms, lies emancipation.

The exoteric Brahman

12. The higher Brahman is converted into the lower Brahman[38] by imposing upon it pure[39] or unsurpassable[40] determinations. The lower Brahman is to be understood in all passages where the Scriptures ascribe any sort of determination, attri-

[36] Ato 'nyad ārtam, *BAU. iii*, 4.2. [37] Antar-ātman.
[38] Aparam brahma. [39] Viçuddha. [40] Niratiçaya.

bute, form, or distinguishing feature to Brahman. This is done not for the sake of cognition, but for purposes of worship,[41] and the fruit of this worship, as well as that of works which belong to the same category, is not emancipation,[42] but happiness,[43] chiefly in heaven, but nevertheless limited to the round-of-rebirths or *saṁsāra*. Heavenly glory,[44] however, attained after death by way of the Path of the Gods,[45] through worship of the lower Brahman, leads to full cognition and hence to complete emancipation. This is called progressive emancipation.[46] Complete emancipation is not its immediate result, since the worshippers of the lower Brahman have not yet wholly burnt away their ignorance. For it is ignorance which determines the higher Brahman and thereby converts it into the lower Brahman. The nature of Brahman is as little changed by being thus determined (to use again the oft-cited simile) as the clearness of the crystal is affected by the colour by which it is tinged, or the sun by its reflections moving on the surface of a body of water, or space by bodies burnt in it or moving in it.

The elaborately developed conceptions of the lower Brahman may be divided into three groups according as it is conceived pantheistically as world-soul, psychologically as principle of the individual soul, or theistically as a personal God.

[41] Upāsanā. [42] Mokṣa, niḥçreyasa. [43] Abhyudaya.
[44] Āiçvarya. [45] Devayāna. [46] Krama-mukti.

13. Several of the most important of the passages that constitute the first group may here be mentioned.

The exoteric Brahman as world-soul

At ChU. iii. 14, Brahman is called "all-effecting, all-wishing, all-smelling, all-tasting (that is, the principle of all action and sensuous perception), embracing the universe, silent, unperturbed."[47] Again, the moon and sun are called its eyes, the four quarters of the sky its ears, the wind its breath,[48] and so forth. To this class, also, belong such passages as represent Brahman as the source of all light;[49] as the light beyond the heavens and in the heart;[50] as the ether from which all creatures proceed,[51] and which differentiates names and forms;[52] as the vital principle

[47] "*Verily this universe is Brahman; in silence one should think it as beginning, ending, and breathing in him (the Brahman). Now man is formed out of will. According to what his will is in this world, so he will be when he has departed; let him then seek (the good) will. Spirit is his substance, life is his body, light is his form, his thoughts are truth, his self is infinity. All-effecting, all-wishing, all-smelling, all-tasting, embracing the universe, silent, unperturbed—this is myself in the inner heart, smaller than a kernel of rice, smaller than a grain of barley, smaller than a mustard seed, smaller than a grain of millet, even than a husked grain of millet—this is myself in the inner heart, greater than the earth, greater than the sky, greater than heaven, greater than all these worlds. The all-effecting, all-wishing, all-smelling, all-tasting, embracing the universe, silent, unperturbed—this is myself in the inner heart, this is the Brahman. When I shall depart from here I shall enter into it. He who knows this has no doubt. Thus spake Çāṇḍilya; thus spake Çāṇḍilya.*" *This is the well-known doctrine of Çāṇḍilya in the Chāndogya-Upanishad, iii.* 14.

[48] *MuU. ii.* 1.1. [49] *MuU. ii.* 2.10; *KthU. v.* 15; *ÇvetU. vi.* 14.

[50] *ChU. iii.* 13.7. [51] *ChU. i.* 9.1.

[52] "*It is the ether which expands names and forms: that wherein they*

from which all creatures spring,[53] and in which the entire world moves trembling;[54] as the inward ruler;[55] as the principle of the world-order, the bridge which keeps these worlds asunder so that they are not confounded;[56] and as the power by which sun and moon, heaven and earth, minutes, hours, years, and days remain discrete;[57] finally as the world-destroyer who reabsorbs all created things.[58]

14. Frequently contrasted with the vast spatial extent which the preceding conceptions suggest are the minute

both are is the Brahman, the Immortal, the Self. I go forth to the hall of the Lord of Creatures, to his house (this world). I am the glory of the Brahmans, the glory of the warriors, the glory of the husbandmen. To the glory I have attained. May I, the glory of glory, never go to the gray, toothless (a human body)." *ChU. viii.* 14.1.

53 *ChU. i.* 11.5.

54 *KthU. vi.* 1.

55 *BAU. iii.* 7.3.

56 *ChU. viii.* 4.1–2.

57 "*This it is, O Gārgī, that the Brāhmaṇas call the Imperishable. It is neither coarse nor subtile, neither short nor long, neither red (like fire) nor fluid (like water), neither shadowy nor dark, neither wind nor ether, not adherent, without taste, without smell, without eye and without ear, without speech, without understanding, without vigour and without breath, without mouth and without measure, without inner or outer; it devours nothing and is devoured by no one. By the command of that Imperishable, O Gārgī, sun and moon stand apart. By the command of that Imperishable, O Gārgī, heaven and earth stand apart. By the command of that Imperishable, O Gārgī, what are called minutes and hours, days and nights, half-months, months, seasons, years, all stand apart. By the command of that Imperishable, O Gārgī, some streams flow to the East from the snow-mountains, others to the West, or to any other quarter. By the command of that Imperishable, O Gārgī, men praise the generous, the gods follow the sacrificer, the fathers the libation for the dead.*" *BAU. iii.* 9.8–9.

58 *KthU. ii.* 25.

dimensions attributed to Brahman as psychical principle. As such it abides in the citadel of the body;[59] in the lotus of the heart;[60] as a dwarf;[61] as tall as a single span;[62] or an inch;[63] smaller than a grain of millet;[64] as big as the point of an awl;[65] as vital principle;[66] as spectator;[67] also as the man in the eye.[68] Illustrations of this sort might be multiplied.

The exoteric Brahman as individual soul

15. These conceptions of the conditioned Brahman culminate in the conception of him as Īçvara, that is, as a personal God. In the Upanishads we find this view comparatively seldom and less fully developed,[69] but in the Vedānta system it plays an important part. On Īçvara's consent depends the round-of-rebirths, and on his grace[70] depends that true knowledge which brings emancipation. Just as rain develops each plant from seed, each after its own kind, so Içvara, guided by the deeds done in the previous existence, and making the conditions of the new life to proceed from these deeds, decrees to souls both what they are to do and what they are to experience. It must be borne in mind, however, that the personification of Brahman as Īçvara, as Ruler, in contrast to the world

The exoteric Brahman as personal God

[59] *PU. v.* 5.
[60] *ChU. viii.* 1.1.
[61] *KthU. v.* 3.
[62] *ChU. v.* 18.1.
[63] *KthU. iv.* 12.
[64] *ChU. iii.* 14.3.
[65] *ÇvetU. v.* 8.
[66] *KshU. iii. 2 and* 8.
[67] *MuU. iii.* 1.1.
[68] *ChU. i.* 7.6; *iv.* 15.1.
[69] *See Içā*, 1; *BAU. iv.* 4.22; *KshU. iii.* 8; *KthU. ii.* 4.12.
[70] Prasāda, anugraha.

over which he is to rule, is confined to the empirical point of view. This view, based on ignorance, has in the strict sense no reality.[71]

[71] *BAU. ii.* 4.13.

CHAPTER III

COSMOLOGY

16. THE duality of teachings[1] in theology, and, as we shall see, in eschatology, corresponds to two different points of view, one view in the province of cosmology, and the other in that of psychology. The first of these, the empirical point of view,[2] teaches the creation of the world by Brahman and the transmigration of souls invested with the *upadhis* and thus made individual. The second, the metaphysical point of view,[3] maintains the identity of the soul and Brahman, denies all manifoldness, and in so doing denies not only the creation and existence of the world, but also individuality and transmigration of souls. Greatly to the detriment of clearness and consistency, this distinction is not everywhere strictly observed in the cosmology and in the psychology. The system is, in general, treated from the metaphysical point of view to the neglect of the empirical, without, however, denying, or being able to deny, to the latter its relative justification, since it is the necessary postulate of the *aparā vidyā* of the eschatology. In consequence of this, the creation of the world is treated at length and in very realistic fashion in the cosmology; but we are nevertheless constantly meeting with the assertion that this teaching of

Empirical and metaphysical points of view

[1] Aparā *and* parā vidyā.

[2] Vyavahāra-avasthā, *literally, point of view of practical life.*

[3] Paramārtha-avasthā, *literally, point of view of highest reality.*

the Scriptures in regard to the creation is merely intended to enforce the doctrine of the Brahmanhood of the world, and that for this reason only has the conception of causality been substituted for that of identity. In the psychology, the metaphysical doctrine of the identity of Brahman and the world is maintained throughout, and is defended against the opposite empirical point of view presupposed in eschatology. At times, however, the metaphysical doctrine gives way before the empirical, as, for instance, in maintaining the coming into being of souls. Since, however, the arguments of the empirical point of view apply to a part of the exposition only, a clear presentation of the empirical psychology is lacking. Nevertheless, we may get a correct idea of this side of the system from the consideration of incidental and scattered remarks.

The relation of the esoteric and exoteric teachings to the metaphysical and empirical point of view

17. The consistency of the system requires that the higher knowledge in theology and eschatology, together with the metaphysical point of view in cosmology and psychology, should make one inseparable metaphysical system. Also it requires that the lower knowledge of the theology and eschatology should unite with the empirical point of view of the cosmology and psychology to form a general presentation of metaphysics as it appears from the empirical point of view of *avidyā* (that is, realism), and that this empirical metaphysics

should constitute a system of popular religion for the use of all those who cannot rise to the point of view of identity. Above all, it is plain that only the lower and not the higher Brahman can be conceived as the creator of the universe, chiefly because, for creation, as is repeatedly asserted, a multiplicity of faculties is needed.[4] Such a multiplicity, however, is predicated only of the lower Brahman. And, indeed, the passage which enumerates such a multiplicity of creative faculties, "he is all-effecting, all-wishing, all-smelling, all-tasting,"[5] is by preference cited as a proof-text in favour of the doctrine of the lower Brahman.

World-periods

18. According to the Upanishads,[6] Brahman creates the world, and then enters it through the individual soul.[7] There is no mention either of the existence of the individual soul before the creation of the

[4] *This multiplicity of powers appears to be inconsistent with the omnipotence of Brahman expressed in such statements as "all-effecting, all-wishing," and so forth. These powers, without which he could not create or be the cause of the beginning, preservation, or destruction of the world, are inferred from the multiplicity of effects. The relation of these powers to Brahman appears to be that they are immanent in him. He is filled with powers. There is some similarity with the Platonic ideas. One particular power creates and orders the world as a whole. The present world of names and forms, in undeveloped form, is latent in this original power. Particular souls, names and forms, are identical with the multiplex developed states of this latent power. The constant factor running through the cycles of recreated worlds is due to this power in Brahman. The multiple factor must also be in him.*

[5] *ChU. iii.* 14.2.

[6] *ChU. vi.* 3.2; *TS. ii.* 6; *BAU. i.* 4.7; *KshU. iv.* 20.

[7] Anena jīvena ātmanā.

world, or of a creation periodically repeated. In this conception, the germs of the empirical and of the metaphysical doctrines of the Vedānta system lie side by side as yet undeveloped. The metaphysical element is the identity of the soul and Brahman; the empirical element, the unfolding of the world of sense. In the Vedānta system these two doctrines are entirely separate. On the metaphysical side we have identity of the soul and Brahman, but no beginning nor persistence nor dissolution of the world. On the empirical side we have a creation of the universe, but no identity of Brahman and the soul; for the individual soul, with the *upādhis* which make it individual, exists from eternity, and transmigrates, except in case of emancipation, from one body to another for all eternity. The doctrine of the creation of the universe is, however, transformed into a periodical and alternating unfolding of the world from Brahman and reabsorption of the same into Brahman, each cycle repeating itself not once, but countless times through all eternity.

The Souls, as well as the elements, at the reabsorption of the world into Brahman exist potentially as germs in latent power, and at each new creation come forth from him unchanged. In this new conception the original meaning of the doctrine of creation is entirely abandoned, but in the form just indicated the dogma is retained because the Veda teaches it. In the Vedānta system itself there is no motive for a creation of the universe, but rather for its existence from eternity; instead of this, in accordance with the authority of the Scriptures, we find a periodic creation and reabsorption, a cycle which must repeat itself without ceasing and without changing the stability of the universe. For the system demands the eternal existence of the world,—an existence depending, as we shall see, on a moral necessity.

The world is without beginning

19. The leading idea of the empirical cosmology and psychology is the existence from eternity of the round-of-rebirths.[8] Without beginning there has existed, separately from Brahman, a multiplicity of individual souls. These souls are distinguished from Brahman, with whom metaphysically they are identical, by the *upādhis* in which they are enveloped. Among these *upādhis*, which together with the deeds adhere to the soul, must be counted the psychical organs[9] of the subtile body[10] which supports them, and also, occasionally, in a wider sense, the gross body and the external objects. Only the gross body is destroyed in death; the subtile body, with the psychical organs, has existed as the investment of the soul from eternity, and accompanies it in all its transmigrations. The transmigrating soul is also accompanied by the deeds, ritual and moral, which it has done during life, and these prevent the round-of-rebirths from coming to an end; for

[8] Saṁsāra. [9] Indriya, manas, mukhya prāṇa.
[10] Sūkṣma çarīra.

every deed, good as well as bad, demands in compensation reward or punishment, and this not only in another world, but in the form of a subsequent earthly existence. Without deeds no human life is possible; hence no life is possible which is not followed by another as its atonement. Very good deeds produce existence as a god; very bad deeds produce existence as an animal or plant. Even if in this life the soul should not act at all, it would not thereby be preserved from subsequent rebirths, since deeds of remarkable goodness or badness demand several successive births as an atonement. This is the reason why the round-of-rebirths extends through all spheres of existence, from the gods down to plants, without beginning, and, unless the latent power of deeds is consumed by knowledge, also without end.

Moral necessity for the repeated creations of the world

20. The unfolding of the perceptible world[11] is, in its essence, nothing more than the fruit of deeds imposed[12] upon the soul. The world is, as the common formula[13] runs, "retribution of the deed visited upon the doer," it is "that which is to be enjoyed" (*bhogya*); whereas the soul in it is "the enjoyer" (*bhoktar*), and "the doer" (*kartar*), both of them corresponding necessarily and exactly to its "condition of being a doer," that is, to its *katṛtva* or to its activity

[11] Nāma-rūpa-prapañca.

[12] Adhyāropita: *see Shankara on iv.* 1.2; 3.14.

[13] Kriyā-kāraka-phala: *see Shankara on i.* 3.22; 3.18; *ii.* 1.14: *iii.* 4.16.

in the previous existence. The connecting link between the deeds and their fruit—the latter comprising action and suffering in the subsequent existence—is not an invisible power or *adṛṣṭa* of deeds, reaching beyond existence, or at least not that alone; but it is rather the *Īçvara*, a personification of Brahman valid only for the empirical point of view,[14] who retributes action and suffering to the soul in the new birth, according to the deeds done in the previous existence.

The recreation of the world after its absorption into Brahman depends each time upon the same necessity as the succession of rebirths. For souls, although absorbed into Brahman, still persist, together with their deeds, in a latent state as germs, and the latter demand for their atonement the repeated creation of the universe, that is, the unfolding of the elements from Brahman. We will now consider this process in detail.

Inorganic nature: the elements

21. At the time of creation, *sṛṣṭi*, which, according to the meaning of this word, must be conceived as an "outpouring" or emanation, the *ākāça* (the ether, or, more correctly, the all-penetrating visible space conceived as a very subtile matter) comes forth from Brahman first. From the ether comes wind;[15] from wind comes fire;[16] from fire comes water;[17] from water comes earth.[18] In this process the subsequent element is brought forth each time, not by means of

[14] *See paragraph* 15.

[15] Vayu.

[16] Agni, tejas.

[17] Āpas.

[18] Pṛthivī, anna.

the elements themselves, but by Brahman in the form of the elements. In reverse order, at the dissolution of the world earth merges into water, water into fire, fire into wind, wind into ether, ether into Brahman.

The ether is perceived through the sense of hearing; wind, through hearing and touch; fire, through hearing and touch and sight; water, through hearing and touch, sight and taste; and earth, through hearing and touch and sight and taste and smell. The elements, however, as they occur, are not the pure original elements, but a mixture of them, each with a preponderance of one or the other.[19]

Organic nature: souls

22. After Brahman has created the elements, he enters into them, according to the Upanishads, by means of individual souls; that is, according to the system which we are here considering, the transmigrating souls, which even after the dissolution of the world have persisted potentially,[20] awake from this "deep sleep"[21] which is part of the illusion of empirical reality, and receive, in accordance with their deeds in the previous existence, the body of a god or a human being or an animal or a plant. The process is as follows: the seed of the elements which souls carry with them in their transmigrations, in the form of the subtile

[19] *A systematic exposition of this theory of the blending of the elements is not found in Shankara's Commentary on the Brahmasūtras, but only later in the Vedāntasāra.*

[20] Çakti-ātmanā. [21] Māyāmayī mahāsuṣupti: *see Shankara on i.* 4.3.

body, grows through the accretion of similar particles proceeding from the gross elements to the gross body;[22] at the same time the psychical organs,[23] which were all implicated[24] during the transmigration, unfold themselves.[25]

The body is "the complex of organs of activity built up of names and forms;"[26] it is, then, a complex of elements; the soul is the lord (*svāmin*) of this complex. The growth of the body arises from the elements of which three parts, gross, middle, and subtile, are distinguished. In correspondence with this tripartite division, faeces and flesh and *manas* come from the earth; urine and blood and *prāṇa* come from water; bones and marrow and speech come from fire. Since, however, according to this system, the soul has already brought its psychical organs with it, and among them, *manas* and *prāṇa* and speech, we must either admit an inconsis-

[22] *Cause and effect are identical not only in unalterable substances, but also in substances which are perceived to change. The substance milk is the same whether in the form of curds or of butter or of ghee. Certain particles of a permanent substance become more or less evident, as the case may be. There is no transition from being to not-being. The baby is not different in substance from the youth, or the boy from the aged man. Similarly, gross elements in our body remain unchanged in substance when they become a part of the physical frame, and also when the body is resolved again into its elements.*

[23] Mukhya prāṇa, manas, indriya. [24] Sampiṇḍita.

[25] *What happens to the organs of the souls of plants is not said; we may assume that they remain implicated.*

[26] Nāma-rūpa-kṛta-kārya-karaṇa-saṁghāta: *see Shankara on ii.* 1.22; 1.14; 3.43.

tency, or else assume that the growing *manas* and *prāṇa* and speech bear the same relation to the innate psychical organs of like name that the gross body does to the subtile one. The evolution of these substances from nourishment is made possible by the fact that each body[27] contains all the original elements of nature.

According to their origin, organisms are divided into those sprung from germs (plants), those sprung from moisture (insects), those born from an egg, and those born alive. Procreation takes place as follows: the soul of the child entering the father through the medium of nourishment remains in him only as a guest, and passing over through the medium of sperma to the body of the mother, develops, by the aid of her blood, the subtile body into the gross body. Death is the separation of the soul, together with its organs and with the subtile body, from the gross body; the organism is destroyed, and the soul proceeds on its further migration. The length of life is not a matter of chance, but is exactly predetermined by the quantity of deeds to be expiated, just as the nature of the life is predetermined by their quality. However, there are deeds which cannot be expiated in one life, but only by a series of births. Only such deeds, for instance, explain why a soul does not stop migrating when it enters a plant. Since each plant is an incarnated soul, and each incarnation serves

[27] *See paragraph* 21.

the purpose of an expiation, the system proceeds logically in attributing sensation to plants also.[28]

Although the life of the souls of plants and of animals and of human beings is of short duration, those souls which, by reason of superior achievements in a previous existence, have been born as gods are deathless, that is, they persist until the next dissolution of the world. Then they too revert to the round-of-rebirth, and the places of Indra and others may next time be filled by other souls.[29]

Non-existence of the world from the metaphysical point of view

23. As all clay vessels are in reality clay, and as the conversion of clay into vessels, "depending on words only," is "but a name," [30] so the whole universe is in fact only Brahman, and apart from Brahman [31] has no existence; there is nothing separate from Brahman.[32]

Here our system goes further than the Veda. The

[28] *See Shankara on iii.* 1.24.

[29] *The gods are mortal. The Vedas are eternal. The Vedas speak of the gods. Why then are not the gods eternal? The words of the Vedas are eternal; but the objects to which they refer are not the individual, but the species. The word "Indra" refers not to the individual, but to a particular position* (sthāna). *Whoever holds this position bears the name. The distinction is between the individual, the manifestation* (vyakti), *and the species, the form* (ākriti). *These species, like Plato's* εἶδος, *become powers* (çakti, δύναμις). *From them the worlds are re-created after a world-dissolution.*

[30] Vācārambhanaṁ vikāro, nāmadheyam, *ChU. vi.* 1.4. *Compare the saying of Parmenides,* Τῷ πάντ' ὄνομ' ἐστίν, ὅσσα βροτοὶ κατέθεντο, πεποιθότες εἶναι ἀληθῆ.

[31] Brahma-vyatirekeṇa.

[32] Na iha nānā asti kiṁcana, *BAU. iv.* 4.19.

whole unfolding of names and forms,[33] the whole complex of phenomena,[34] when we regard it from the point of view of ultimate reality [35] is created, maintained, and imposed upon the soul by ignorance,[36] springs from false cognition,[37] and is mere false supposition [38] which is to be disproved by complete cognition;[39] just as the illusion that a rope is a snake, or that the trunk of a tree is a man, or that a mirage is an expanse of water, is disproved on closer examination and disappears. The whole world is only an illusion[40] which Brahman as magician[41] evolves[42] from himself, and by which he is no more affected than is the magician by the illusion which he has produced. To use a variation of this simile, Brahman is made to appear multiplex[43] by ignorance[44] just as is the magician by his magic. Brahman is the cause of the persistence of the world just as the magician is the cause of the illusion which he produces; and he is the cause of the reabsorption of the world into himself[45] just as, in similar fashion, the earth absorbs creatures into itself.

The variety of action[46] during the persistence of the world, and the variety of potential existence[47] before and after the world's phenomenal appearance, both rest on ignorance or false cognition. The conception of *avidyā*

[33] Nāmarūpa-prapañca. [34] Rūpa-bheda. [35] Paramārtha-avasthā.
[36] Avidyā-kalpita, avidyā-pratyupasthāpita, avidyā-adhyāropita.
[37] Mithyājñāna-vijṛmbhita. [38] Abhimāna. [39] Saṁyag-darçana.
[40] Māyā. [41] Māyāvin. [42] Prasārayati. [43] Vibhāvyate.
[44] Avidyā. [45] Sva-ātmani eva upasaṁhāra-kāraṇam.
[46] Bheda-vyavahāra. [47] Bheda-çakti.

or *mithyā jñāna* bars the way to all further investigation. We cannot answer the question which is innate in all of us, the question, Whence arises this ignorance? The deepest explanation lies perhaps in the oft-recurring simile of a man who, through defective vision, sees two moons when in fact there is but one In general, the non-existence of the universe is a relative non-existence only. The multiplex of phenomena, the universe of names and forms, the illusion (*māyā*), cannot be said to be the same as Brahman (*tat*), nor yet to be different (*anya*) from him.[48] Like visions in a dream, the names and forms are true (*satya*) so long only as the dream lasts, and no longer true when the sleep comes to an end.

This idealism which we see first appearing in the Upanishads, the Vedānta tries to bring into agreement with the Vedic doctrine of creation, by maintaining that creation signifies only the identity [49] of the universe and of Brahman; that the world is the effect and that Brahman is the cause, but that cause and effect are identical, —a thesis for the proof of which the persistence of substance in changes of its qualities serves as chief argument.

[48] Tattva-anyatvābhyām anirvacanīya.

[49] Ananyatva, tādātmya.

CHAPTER IV

PSYCHOLOGY

24. ALTHOUGH we are persuaded that all the complex of phenomena spread before us, all names and forms of which the world is composed, are an illusion resting on ignorance, comparable to the illusion of a dream, still there is one point in the universe where this view is not applicable. This point is our own soul, our true self.[1] This self cannot be demonstrated because it is the presupposition of every demonstration; but also it cannot be disproved because even the denial implies an affirmation of it.[2]

The soul alone real

What now is the nature of this sole basis of all certainty, of the soul, of our inner self? How is it related to Brahman who comprehends all existence in himself?

25. The soul cannot be different from Brahman because there is nothing existing beyond Brahman. It is

[1] *Or* ātman.

[2] "*If the Self were a modification of something else, it would be a mere effect. But just because it is the Self, it is impossible for us to entertain the idea of its being capable of refutation. For the knowledge of the Self is not adventitious, not established by any so-called means of right knowledge; it is rather self-established. The Self, the abode of the power which acts through the means of right knowledge, is established previously to that knowledge. And to refute such a self-established entity is impossible. An adventitious thing may be refuted, but not that which is the essential nature (of him who attempts the refutation); for it is the essential nature of him who refutes. The heat of the fire is not sublated by the fire itself.*"

This form of the Cogito ergo sum *is found in Shankara on Vedānta Sūtra, ii. 3.7.*

not, however, to be considered as a transformation of Brahman, because Brahman is unchangeable. Neither is it a part of Brahman, since Brahman has no parts. There remains then only the assumption that the soul is identical with Brahman; that each one of us is himself the whole, indivisible, immutable, all-pervading Brahman.

The soul identical with Brahman

26. From this it follows that everything established in regard to the nature of the higher Brahman applies also to the soul. As Brahman is in essence pure intelligence,[3] so is the soul also; and to it apply equally all those negative predicates the object of which is to keep away from Brahman all determinations which could limit his being. According to this, the soul is, like Brahman, omnipresent,[4] or, as we might say, superspatial, all-knowing and all-powerful, neither acting[5] nor enjoying[6] nor suffering.

The soul from the metaphysical point of view

27. If this is the true nature of the soul, it follows that everything which is at variance with this nature is merely "attributed" to the soul through ignorance. To such attributes or *upādhis*, which depend on false cognition only and which include all physical existence, the following facts are due. First, that the soul while in the state of *samsāra* is not all-pervasive and omnipresent, but dwells in the limited space of the *manas* within the heart. Second,

The soul from the empirical point of view

[3] Cāitanya. [4] Vibhu, sarvagata. [5] Kartar. [6] Bhoktar.

that it is not all-knowing and all-powerful, since through the *upādhis* its original omniscience and omnipotence become latent, just as light and heat of the fire are latent in wood. Finally, that through its union with the *upādhis*, the soul becomes an actor and enjoyer; and by these latter qualities its entanglement in the *saṁsāra* is necessitated; for the deeds of one life must be requited by enjoyment and action in the next succeeding life. The action, again, which forms a part of that requital, requires in turn a new requital, and so on to infinity.

28. This round-of-rebirth (*saṁsāra*), without beginning and without end, rests wholly on the fact that the soul's true nature is hidden from it by the limiting conditions (*upādhis*) imposed upon it by ignorance (*avidyā*). Among these *upādhis*, which convert Brahman into the individual soul together with the activities and sensations of the soul, the gross body, together with all the things and relations of the external world, is not included. The gross body is resolved at death into the elements. The *upādhis* consist of the following:

Limiting conditions

First, the *manas* and the *indriya;*

Second, the *mukhya prāṇa;*

Third, the *sūkṣma çarīra.*

To this permanent psychical equipment, with which the soul remains endowed from eternity and until emancipation, there is added a fourth variable element which we may call the moral qualification. We will now consider these *upādhis* in detail.

Mind and sense-organs

29. Though the gross body[7] and its organs,[8] the eye, ear, hands, feet, and so forth, perish with death, the functions[9] of these organs, conceived as self-existent essences, remain bound up with the soul for all time. These are the *indriya*, the senses, which the soul puts forth as tentacles during life and at death draws back into itself. Upon these depend the two sides of conscious life, perception and action Corresponding to these two sides, the soul has five perceptive faculties,[10] seeing, hearing, smelling, tasting, and touch; and five faculties relating to action,[11] grasping, moving, speaking, generating and voiding. These ten *indriya*, which are usually denoted by the names of the corresponding organs of the gross body, are governed by a central organ, the *manas*, which transforms into representations the data supplied by the perceptive faculties[12] and effects the accomplishment of volitions through the faculties of action. It consequently represents both what we call understanding and what we call conscious will. The *indriya* permeate the whole body, but the *manas* dwells, "having the size of an awl's point," in the heart; and in the *manas*, filling it entirely and in closest union, to be sundered only by emancipation, dwells the soul,—the soul

[7] Deha, kārya-karaṇa-saṁghāta. [8] Karaṇa. [9] Vṛtti.
[10] Jñāna-indriya. [11] Karma-indriya.
[12] Manasā hi eva paçyati, manasā çṛṇoti, *BAU. i.* 5.3.

which only through the organs to which it is bound by ignorance becomes actor and enjoyer, but itself stands aloof from all the activity of the organs as pure perception,[13] a passive spectator,[14] so that in spite of its being plunged into the activities of daily life, it remains in its real essence untouched.[15]

30. Less closely than to the *manas* and the *indriya*, the soul seems to be attached to the *mukhya prāṇa*, a term, which in the Upanishads, still denotes "breath in the mouth;" whereas in the Vedānta system it has come to mean "the chief breath of life." As the *manas* and the *indriya* are functions of perception and action hypostasized as special entities, so the *mukhya prāṇa*, on which they all depend, is a hypostasis of the physical life itself which is regulated through this *mukhya prāṇa* in its five branches, *prāṇa*, *apāna*, *vyāna*, *samāna*, *udāna*. Of these, *prāṇa* regulates expiration; *apāna* inspiration. *Vyāna* is that which maintains life while breathing is momentarily suspended; *samāna* is the digestive principle, and just as these four cause the persistence of life, so *udāna* causes its end by leading the soul out of the body at death through one of the one hundred and one principal veins. Along with the soul the *manas*, *indriya* and *mukhya prāṇa* leave the body. As during life they are the forces which govern the organs of the body, so after the death of the body they are the

Vital principle

[13] Upalabdhi. [14] Sākṣin. [15] Asaṅga, ananvāgata.

germ from which at each new birth the organs of the body grow anew.

31. As the soul carries with it the germ of the physical organs in the *indriya*, so it carries the germ of the body itself in the *sūkṣma çarīra*, or, as it is described more explicitly by Shankara, "the subtile parts of the elements forming the germ of the body."[16] How these subtile parts of the elements are related to the gross body is not more definitely determined. The subtile body composed of them possesses materiality,[17] but also transparency;[18] hence it is not seen in the soul's migration. From it is derived animal warmth. The coldness of the dead body arises from the fact that the subtile body has left it at the same time as the other organs, to accompany the soul in its transmigrations.

Subtile body (*sūkṣma çarīra*)

32. To the psychical organism[19] which adheres to the soul at all times in life and in death, and which appears always unchangeable, there is attached further, escorting the soul in its migration, a variable *upādhi*. This is the moral qualification consisting in the store of deeds[20] collected during life. Besides the physical substrate,[21] that is, the subtile body, this goes out with the soul as a moral substrate[22]

The moral qualification

[16] Deha-bījāni bhūta-sukṣmāni. *According to Shankara, in his comment on iii.* 1.2, *the elements already mixed are meant. A contrary interpretation is given in Vedānta-sāra, lxxvii.*

[17] Tanutva.

[18] Svacchatva.

[19] Manas, indriya, mukhya-prāṇa, sūkṣma çarīra.

[20] Karma-ācaya.

[21] Bhūta-āçraya.

[22] Karma-āçraya.

and absolutely conditions the future existence in enjoyment and suffering as well as in action.

33. There are four states of the migratory soul: waking, dreaming, a state of deep sleep, and death. In the waking state, the soul, which in union with the *manas* dwells in the heart, rules the whole body, perceiving and acting through the medium of the *manas* and the *indriya*. In dreaming, the *indriya* are at rest, but the *manas* still remains active, and the soul, surrounded by the *manas* and the *indriya* which have entered the *manas*, circulates by means of the veins in the body, and while doing so sees dream-pictures built up of waking impressions.[23] In deep sleep the connection of the soul with the *manas* is broken; the *manas* and *indriya*, having come to rest, enter the veins or the pericardium, and thence enter the *mukhya prāṇa*, the activity of which continues even in deep sleep. The soul, thus temporarily freed from all these *upādhis*, enters by means of the ether of the heart into Brahman. Since, apart from the *upādhis*, the soul is Brahman, this entrance into Brahman is merely another expression of complete emancipation from the *upādhis*. On waking, the soul goes forth from this temporary identification with Brahman with all its individual limitations, exactly as it was before.

Special states of the soul

[23] Vāsanā.

CHAPTER V

MIGRATION OF THE SOUL

34. At death, the *indriya* first enter the *manas;* the *manas* then enters the *mukhya prāṇa;* the *mukhya prāṇa* enters the soul to which is adhering the moral qualification; the soul then enters the *sūkṣma çarīra.* After all these have come together in the heart, the point of the heart becomes luminous in such wise as to light up the path, and the *udāna* escorts the soul with the *upādhis* from the body. From the body of those possessing the lower knowledge, the soul goes through the artery of the head;[1] from the body of the ignorant, it goes through the hundred other principal veins of the body. The soul of a person possessing the higher knowledge, as we shall see, does not go out at all. Beginning at this point, the paths divide. The performer of pious works goes upon the path of the fathers (*pitṛ-yāna*); the man possessing the lower knowledge, upon the path of the gods (*devayāna*); he who is without knowledge and without pious works, that is, the bad man, remains shut out from both these paths.

Departure of the soul from body

35. The path of the fathers, which is destined for those who possess neither the higher nor the lower knowledge of Brahman, but who have done good deeds, leads the soul in compensation up to the moon. The stations on this road

Destiny of the doer of pious works

[1] Mūrdhanyā nādī, *later called* suṣumnā.

are as follows: smoke; night; the part of the month in which the moon wanes; the part of the year in which the days shorten; the world of the fathers; the ether; the moon. In the heaven of the moon the souls enjoy intercourse with the gods as reward for their deeds. This intercourse lasts till the deeds are consumed. However, only a portion of deeds are thus rewarded by enjoyment on the moon; another portion is left over as a remainder,[2] and finds its recompense in the succeeding birth. In which category any particular deed is to be classed is not made clear. After all the deeds which find their recompense on the moon are consumed, the soul descends again. As stations on the return there are named: ether; wind; smoke; clouds; rain; plants; the sperma; the womb. At all these stations the soul remains only temporarily, and must be distinguished from the elements and souls through which it passes. Finally, after it has arrived in the womb corresponding to its deeds, it comes forth to another life on earth.

Destiny of the wicked. Hell and the third place

36. The wicked, who have neither knowledge nor deeds, do not ascend to the moon. Their fate is not clearly traced, since Shankara in one place refers to a punishment in the seven hells of Yama; in another, to the "third place" in which these souls are born as lower animals. Although the wicked are excluded from life on the moon, not all souls

[2] Anuçaya.

which return from there obtain a happy life. Some, owing to good conduct, are destined to be born again in one of the three higher castes, but others, owing to bad conduct, enter the bodies of Caṇḍālas and animals. A reduction of these statements to a consistent whole, which could easily have been brought about by distinguishing different grades in the good and bad deeds to be atoned for, is not made in the work of Shankara.

Destiny of pious worshippers of Brahman

37. From those who perform religious works[3] prescribed in the old Vedic sacrificial cult, must be distinguished those who adhere to the doctrine of Brahman, but nevertheless cannot raise themselves to a right knowledge of the dogma of identity, and accordingly know Brahman, not as their own soul, but as a god different from themselves whom they worship. These possessors of the lower knowledge,[4] that is, worshippers of the lower, conditioned Brahman, all, with the exception of those who have worshipped him under a symbol (*pratīka*), go after death by the path of the gods into the lower Brahman. The stations of this path are differently designated in the different accounts. Shankara interweaves them into a whole. According to the Chāndogya Upanishad[5] the following regions are traversed by the soul of the man possessing

[3] *See paragraph* 35.

[4] *Lower knowledge is* apara vidyā; *lower, conditioned Brahman is* apara saguṇa.

[5] *With variations in BAU. and in KshU.*

the lower knowledge after it has passed out of the body through the artery of the head: the flames of the fire; the day; the part of the month in which the moon waxes; the part of the year in which the days lengthen; the year;[6] the sun; the moon; the lightning. These stations are not to be considered either as signposts or as places of enjoyment for the soul, but as guides which it needs because it cannot use its own organs, which are in an enveloped condition. The guides of the soul hitherto mentioned are to be understood as divine but anthropomorphic beings; later, however, after its entrance into the lightning, the soul is received by a "man who is not like a human being,"[7] and by him is escorted through Varuṇaloka, Indraloka, and Prajāpatiloka into Brahman. Nevertheless, by Brahman is here meant the lower, conditioned Brahman who has been born himself[8] and hence, at the dissolution of the universe, perishes. In the world of this Brahman souls enjoy sovereignty, *āiçvarya*, which consists in an omnipotence like that of a god though restricted to fixed limits, and including the fulfilment of every wish. The *manas* serves as medium of enjoyment. Whether souls also make use of the *indriyas*, which also accompany them, is doubtful. Among their sovereign powers belongs the ability to animate several bodies at once, and they divide themselves among these bodies by means of a division of their *upādhis*. Although for souls

[6] *As variants:* devaloka *or* vāyuloka.

[7] Puruṣo 'mānavaḥ.

[8] Kārya.

which have entered the lower Brahman by the *devayāna*, this *āiçvarya* is finite and lasts only till the dissolution of the universe, still Scripture says of them: "for such there is no return." We must therefore suppose that in the world of Brahman the higher knowledge of the *saṁyag-darçana* is revealed to them, and that at the end of the world, when the lower Brahman also perishes, they enter with him into "eternal and absolute *nirvāṇa.*" This entrance is called progressive emancipation (*kramamukti*); it is performed in progression, or gradual emancipation, because it is obtained by the intermediate grades of heavenly sovereignty. Opposed to this stands the immediate emancipation of the knowing one, which is reached even here on earth, and which we have next to consider.

CHAPTER VI

EMANCIPATION

Emancipation comes from knowledge

38. The question of the possibility of emancipation from individual existence, which serves as the keystone of the Vedānta as of other Indian systems of philosophy, presupposes the pessimistic view that all individual existence is an evil. This thought finds occasional expression in the Veda[1] as well as in the system under consideration,[2] but it is not proclaimed with so much emphasis as we should expect.

How, then, is an emancipation[3] from the bonds[4] of existence possible? Not by works: for these, good as well as bad, demand their requital; necessitate accordingly a new existence, and are the cause of the continuance of the *saṁsāra;* not yet by (moral) purification,[5] for this can take place only in an object capable of change, whereas the *ātman*, the soul, whose emancipation is con-

[1] "*These worlds are in sooth pleasureless*" (anandā nāma te lokah): *see BAU. iv.* 4.11; *also iii.* 4.2; *KthU. i.* 1.3; *Içā*, 3.

[2] "*Mortal surely, O Mighty One, is this body and always beset by death. It is the abode of that Self which is immortal and unembodied. The embodied is beset by pleasure and pain. So long as he is embodied, no repulsion of pleasure and of pain is possible. But the disembodied neither pleasure nor pain affect. Disembodied is the wind; the cloud, the lightning, and the thunder are disembodied. Now as these, arising from the heavenly space, appear in their own form as soon as they have approached the highest light, so this complete satisfaction (of the Self in emancipation) arises out of this body, enters the highest light, and appears in its own form. That is the supreme soul* (uttama puruṣaḥ)." *ChU. viii.* 12.1–3.

[3] Mokṣa. [4] Bandha. [5] Saṁskāra.

cerned, is unchangeable. Emancipation therefore cannot consist in any development or in any activity, but only in the recognition of something already real, still concealed through ignorance. "From knowledge comes emancipation."[6] When once the soul knows its identity with Brahman, this knowledge is emancipation.[7] The individual soul on recognizing its identity with Brahman becomes by that concept the universal spirit.[8]

39. The *ātman*, in the knowledge of which emancipation consists, is nothing else than the knowing subject in us. For this reason it is not knowable by the senses, "ne'er canst thou see the seer of seeing;"[9] it cannot, like an object, be placed before us and examined; knowledge of it cannot be obtained at will, and even searching in the Scripture is not enough to attain this knowledge, but merely serves to remove obstacles. Whether the *ātman* is known or not depends, as does the perception of every object, on one fact, whether it manifests itself to us; depends consequently on the *ātman* itself. Hence in the lower knowledge, which opposes the *ātman* to our own self as a personal god and worships it,[10] knowledge appears as the grace of God. In the higher knowledge, since the

Knowledge by the grace of God

[6] Jñānān mokṣaḥ.

[7] *The saying is "that art thou," not "that shalt thou be." See Shankara, iii.* 3.32.

[8] *See Shankara, i.* 1.4. [9] *BAU. iii.* 4.2. [10] *See paragraph* 15.

ātman is in reality not an object, the cause of its knowledge is not further explicable.

40. In spite of this, religious practice recognizes certain means[11] by which knowledge of the *ātman* may be promoted. From the man who enters upon the pursuit of the higher knowledge there is demanded study of the Veda and the four requisites: distinguishing between eternal and perishable substance; renunciation of the enjoyment of reward here and hereafter; attainment of the six means; longing for emancipation. The six means are, tranquillity; control of passions; renunciation; patient endurance; concentration;[12] and faith.

Aids to the attainment of knowledge

Besides these requisites, commonly enumerated in the instruction of the schools, two other means serve in a general way to promote knowledge: works and meditation.

Works, it is true, do not have a positive, but merely a negative value in the scheme of salvation.[13] They cannot create knowledge, but they aid in acquiring it by destroying the barriers standing in the way of its acquisition. Among such barriers are enumerated various emotional disturbances,[14] such as passionate love, hate, and so forth. The works which serve as a means in the acquisition of knowledge are useful partly in a remoter[15] and partly in a closer[16] sense. As remoter means are enumerated,

[11] Sādhana. [12] Samādhi. [13] *See Shankara on iv.* 1.16.
[14] Kleça. [15] Bāhya. [16] Pratyāsanna.

study of the Veda, sacrifice, almsgiving, penance, and fasting.[17] These are to be pursued only till knowledge is attained. In distinction from these, the closer means are to be continued even after the attainment of knowledge. These are, tranquillity of spirit, control of the passions, renunciation, patience, and composedness.[18]

Besides works, pious meditation[19] serves as a means of acquiring knowledge. It consists in devout contemplation of words of Scripture, for example, the words *tat tvam asi*, and, like the process of threshing, is to be repeated until knowledge appears as its fruit. For this result a longer or a shorter time is required according as a person is subject to mental dullness or doubt. After the acquisition of the higher knowledge meditation is no longer needed since it has attained its end. On the other hand, meditations which are connected with works, as well as those practised in the lower knowledge, are to be continued till death, since the thoughts at the hour of death are of importance in shaping the destiny beyond. For meditation in the service of the higher knowledge the position of the body is of no importance; nor is it so for the performance of works. Meditation practised in the lower knowledge must be carried on not standing or lying, but sitting.

41. Knowledge consists in the immediate perception[20]

[17] *BAU. iv.* 4.22. [18] *BAU. iv.* 4.23. [19] Upāsanā.
[20] Anubhava.

of the identity of the soul with Brahman. For the man who has attained to this perception, and with it to the conviction of the non-reality of the phenomenal world and of the round-of-rebirth, past deeds are annihilated. To him in the future deeds no longer cling. This annihilation, moreover, has reference to good as well as to bad deeds, since both require requital and both cease to exist when the *saṁsāra* ceases. The man possessing knowledge has arrived at the following judgement: "The Brahman who, instead of being in essence an actor and enjoyer, as I once thought him, is in truth in all the past, the present, and the future, a non-actor and a non-enjoyer, this Brahman am I; therefore neither was I formerly an actor and enjoyer, nor am I now, nor shall I ever be."[21] With the recognition of the non-reality of being an actor, is recognized also the non-reality of one's own body, which exists as the fruit of action; hence the man possessing knowledge is as little moved by pain in his own body as by that of another; and he who still feels pain has not yet attained perfect knowledge.

Annihilation of deeds

42. As for the man possessing knowledge there is no longer any world, any body, or any pain, so there are no longer any rules to direct his action. He will not, however, on that account, do evil, for in him has been destroyed that illusion which is the pre-

Abolition of all duties

[21] *See Shankara on iv.* 1.13.

liminary to all action good and bad alike. Whether he continues to act at all is unimportant, since his acts do not belong to him and do not cling to him any longer.

Opportune as it would have been to derive positive moral conduct from the condition just described of the man who knows himself to be the soul of the universe,—conduct expressing itself in works of justice and charity,—and though such a conduct may be derived from the Bhagavadgītā,[22] yet Shankara does not touch this question.

Cause of the persistence of emancipated bodies

43. Knowledge consumes the seed of deeds, so that there is no material left for another birth. On the other hand, knowledge cannot destroy deeds whose seed has already sprung up, namely, those which determine the present course of life. For this reason the body persists for a time even after the awakening[23] has been accomplished, just as the potter's wheel continues to turn after the vessel is completed. Still this persistence is a mere illusion of which the enlightened Sage cannot, indeed, rid himself, but by which on the other hand he can no longer be deceived. Likewise the man with defective vision sees two moons, but knows that in fact there is only one.

Absorption into Brahman

44. When the deeds whose fruit has not yet begun to form, and when those whose fruit is the present existence, have been destroyed by

[22] *xiii.* 27–28. [23] Prabodha.

knowledge, then, at the moment of death, complete and eternal emancipation begins for the enlightened sage: "his vital spirits do not depart, but he is Brahman, and in Brahman is he merged."

As rivers run, and in the ocean
Renouncing name and form from vision vanish,
So names and forms the Enlightened Sage renouncing
Enters great Brahman, the all-embracing Spirit.

THE END